DATE DUE			

614218

978
Fla

Flanagan, Alice K.

The Zunis

THE ZUNIS

A TRUE BOOK

by

Alice K. Flanagan

Children's Press®

A Division of Grolier Publishing

New York London Hong Kong Sydney
Danbury, Connecticut

Young Zuni
dancers

Reading Consultant
Linda Cornwell
Learning Resource Consultant
Indiana Department
of Education

Visit Children's Press on the Internet at:
http://publishing.grolier.com

Library of Congress Cataloging-in-Publication Data

Flanagan, Alice K.
    The Zunis / by Alice K. Flanagan.
        p.   cm. — (A True book)
    Includes index.
    Summary: Examines the history, culture, and society of the Zuni
    Indians, one of the groups of Pueblo Indians living in New Mexico.
    ISBN 0–516–20630–3 (lib. bdg.)   0-516-26389-7 (pbk.)
    1. Zuni Indians—Juvenile literature. [1. Zuni Indians. 2. Indians of
    North America—New Mexico.] I. Title. II. Series
E99.Z9F63   1998
978'.004979—dc21   97–6712
                                                                            CIP
                                                                            AC

Contents

The Zunis live in the dry climate of the Southwest.

People of the High Plateau

In a high desert region of the southwestern United States, a group of American Indians has been living for thousands of years. They are the Zunis (ZOO-nees), one of nineteen Native American groups we call Pueblos (PWEB-los). Although the Zunis belong to

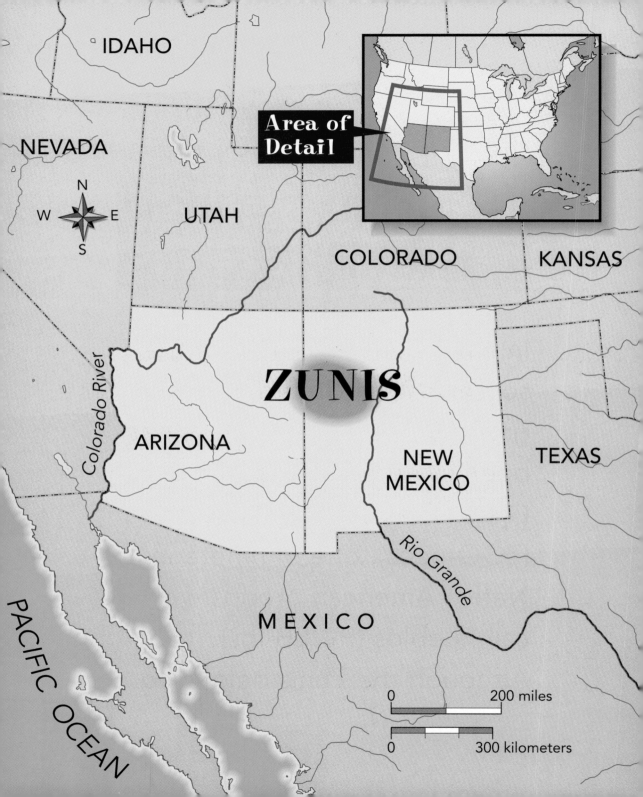

IDAHO

NEVADA

UTAH

Area of Detail

COLORADO

KANSAS

ZUNIS

ARIZONA

NEW
MEXICO

TEXAS

Colorado River

Rio Grande

MEXICO

PACIFIC OCEAN

N
W E
S

0   200 miles

0   300 kilometers

the Pueblo family, the Zunis speak their own language and have customs and beliefs that make them unique.

Today, the Zuni Pueblo is located in northwestern New Mexico, near the Arizona border and the towns of Gallup and Grants. At one time, however, Zuni country included parts of the states of New Mexico, Arizona, Utah, and Colorado.

Proud of an Ancient Past

For generations, the Zunis have built their villages close to the Zuni River and to Corn Mountain (Towayalane), a sacred mountain where their people found safety in earlier times. It is generally believed that the Zunis are the descendants of a prehistoric people

This 1879 photograph shows a Zuni village.
Corn Mountain is on the horizon.

Today, Zuni houses still cluster at the base of Corn Mountain.

called Mogollons (mo-go-YONE), or "Mountain People." The Mogollons lived in southwestern New Mexico and parts of Arizona and northern Mexico thousands of years ago. They were wanderers who moved from season to season, hunting animals and gathering plants for food. They may have been the first people in the Southwest to grow crops and build perma- nent villages near their fields.

Their first homes, called pit houses, were dug three or four feet below the ground and supported by log frames covered by roofs of branches, reeds, and mud. The larger houses, called *kivas*, were

Kivas are used for important religious ceremonies.

used for ceremonies. As set-
tlements grew and people
were influenced by the ideas
of others, they began build-
ing multistoried houses under
natural overhangs of cliffs and
along sheer canyon walls.
Today, in New Mexico,

remains of these early communities are preserved in such places as Chaco Culture National Historical Parks and Bandelier National Monument.

Ancient Mogollon villages are preserved today.

Living in a Sacred Place

The Zunis believe they live in a sacred place. It is the home of their ancestors and where the ancient Spirits dwell. Their creation stories tell of the long struggle their people endured on the journey to their present home.

According to one legend, the Children of the Sun led

Ancestors of the Zunis made this rock drawing centuries ago.

the first people from the underworld. They helped them pass through four worlds, until they finally emerged upon Mother Earth. Then the Spirits sent them south and guided them to the middle of the world—the sacred center where they were meant to dwell. Here, at the center, Zuni ancestors built their first village, called Halona. Now, this is the site of the present Zuni Pueblo.

Great Houses of Stone

In time, other villages spread out from Halona, dotting the valleys and mesa rims. The village built at the top of a mountain later called El Morro was one of the largest. Here, the people lived in an apartment-like structure that contained more than five hundred rooms.

A large Zuni village was built atop the cliffs of El Morro.

The large, communal buildings the Zunis built were made of stone and covered with clay. Built for defense, they had no doors or windows at the ground level. Instead, people entered through holes in the roofs. Rooms were built one on top of the other. They were connected by ladders that were guarded and put away after everyone returned home. The flat roofs served as ceilings for those living below and

The Zunis used ladders to enter and leave their houses.

became floors and yards for the people living on the level above. These were the structures the Zunis were living in when Spaniards invaded their country in 1539. Today, some Zunis still live in these homes.

Clans and Kinship

Families were organized by clans, or groups, and given the names of animals, plants, or elements, such as Eagle, Deer, and Coyote; Corn, Oak, and Cactus; Sun, Water, and Sky. This way of identifying people is still an important part of Zuni culture today.

In the past, Zuni families lived in a series of connected rooms (above). In the Zuni culture today, property and the family name are still passed down through the mother.

Families lived in multistoried housing. Parents and their children shared a single space. Other relatives, such as grandparents, cousins, and aunts and uncles on the mother's side, lived in connecting rooms. The mother, not the father, was head of the household. Property and family name were inherited through her. When her sons married, they went to live with their wives' relatives.

Dancing for Rain

The Zunis are a religious people. Today, and to a greater extent in the past, their daily lives are filled with prayers to the gods, or spirits, who live in everything—humans, plants and animals, clouds and rocks, and man-made things such as baskets

A Zuni elder
chants prayers
during a
ceremony.

Zuni rain dancers

and pots. At the center of their prayers are Mother Earth, who nourishes life, and Father Sky, who provides the sun and sends the rain.

Prayers often take the form of dancing and are accompanied by singing, drumming, and movements that make the spirits and people one. Many of these dances and ceremonies are held in the Zuni Pueblo today, along with celebrations that honor Catholic saints and Spanish feast days. Both are reminders that the Zunis have a respect for their past.

The Shalako

Each year, in late November or early December, clown-like figures called Mud-heads parade through the Zuni Pueblo. They come to announce that the Spirits, in the form of masked

Zuni dancers bring the Shalako into the village.

Festival

dancers called Kachinas, are returning after their long summer absence, and it's time for the Shalako to begin. From earliest times, the Zunis have been celebrating this event. Now, people come from all over the world to pray with the dancers, learn from the clowns, and participate in the ceremonies that bless new homes, bring needed rain, and keep life in balance.

Part of the Shalako festival takes place around a fire.

Three Sisters

For centuries, the Zunis have grown corn, beans, and squash. They call them the "Three Sisters." At one time, the three foods provided most of the Zuni diet. Corn was the main crop. It was boiled, roasted, and crushed. Sometimes it was eaten in

Corn is the main Zuni crop.

stew, or as popcorn, bread, cake, and mush. Corn on the cob was a favorite.

Farming the dry land took great skill and cooperation. Everyone worked together to care for the crops. They dug irrigation ditches from the

river to their fields. Zuni priests held ceremonies throughout the year to pray for rain and to ask the Spirits to bless them with good weather and whatever else they needed for a good harvest of crops.

In the Zuni Pueblo today, farming no longer is the main way people earn a living. Raising livestock and making jewelry, baskets, and pottery for markets around the world are more important.

Today, many Zunis make jewelry for a living.

Zuni Crafts

Like their ancestors, the Zunis weave colorful baskets from plant fibers. The various shapes and designs depict favorite animals or kachinas. Similar images are painted on pottery made from local clay. In the past, painting was done with leaves. Today, artists use

A Zuni woman places clay pots into a fire (left). A finished Zuni clay pot is pictured above.

brushes. In whatever way it is done, the Zunis believe that when something is made, it is given a spirit of its own.

The Zuni women above wear Zuni jewelry made from turquoise and silver. Many Zuni silversmiths are inspired by animals (left).

Zuni artists are known for their beautiful silver and turquoise jewelry. In the past, they borrowed many ideas from their neighbors, the Navajos. Now the Zunis have their own style. They use small sets of turquoise and add shells and a variety of other stones. Making silver jewelry, called silversmithing, is one of the Pueblos' main sources of income.

Under a Zuni Sky

For centuries, the Zuni people have suffered from raids by neighboring tribes and invasions by powerful countries—first by Spain and Mexico and then by the United States. Always, the outsiders threatened to destroy the Zuni way of life, but always it survived.

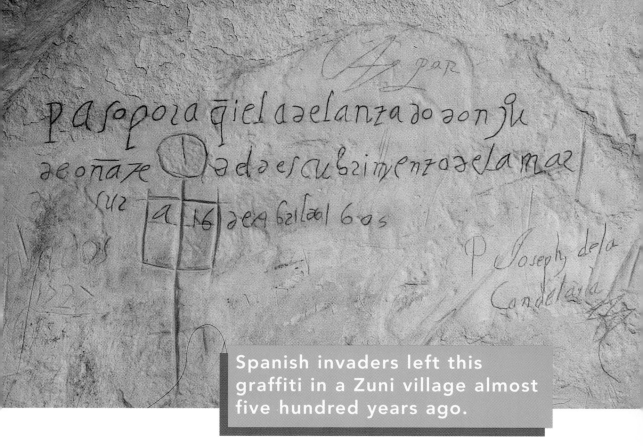

Spanish invaders left this graffiti in a Zuni village almost five hundred years ago.

In 1539, Spanish explorers and Catholic missionaries found the Zunis living in seven villages along the north bank

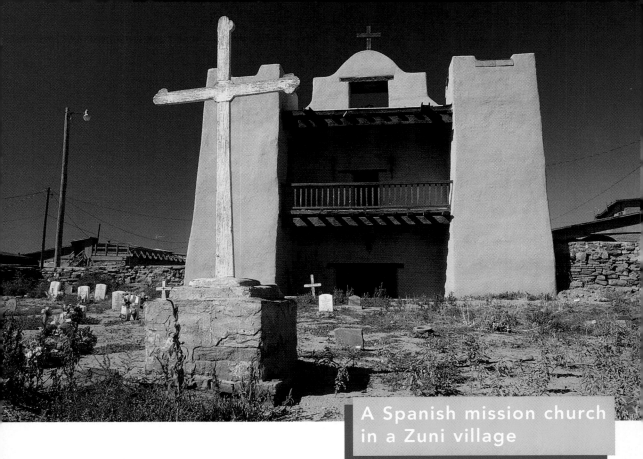

A Spanish mission church in a Zuni village

of the upper Zuni River. They called these towns the Seven Cities of Cibola. For the next 140 years, the Spaniards ruled all the Pueblos. They forced their religion upon the people and tried to make them live like Spaniards. When the missionaries punished the Zunis for following their beliefs, they practiced them secretly.

In 1680, the Zunis joined other Pueblos and drove the Spaniards from their land. But in 1692, Spanish troops and settlers returned. Spain ruled the area of the Southwest until 1821, when Mexico gained its independence from Spain and took control of the area. Then in 1848, Pueblo country became the property of the United States. In 1924, the Zunis and other Native Americans became U.S. citizens.

With each new country that ruled them, the Zunis saw great change. Today, they live in a modern world of computers, VCRs, and the space age. But they listen with their hearts to their ancestors and hold fast to Zuni beliefs and traditions.

Zunis today blend their ancient culture with modern American pop culture.

From both worlds they take what they will need to survive in the 21st century while living in harmony with nature under a Zuni sky.

To Find Out More

Here are some additional resources to help you learn more about the Zunis:

 **Books**

Bartok, Mira, & Christine Ronan. **Pueblo Indians of the Southwest.** Good Year Books, 1995.

Doherty, Craig A. & Katherine M. **The Zunis.** Franklin Watts, 1993.

Flanagan, Alice K. **The Pueblos.** Children's Press, 1998.

Fradin, Dennis. **Sea to Shining Sea: New Mexico.** Children's Press, 1994.

Hallet, Bill & Jill. **Pueblo Indians of New Mexico: Activities and Adventures for Children.** Look & See, 1991.

Hoyt-Goldsmith, Diane. **Pueblo Storyteller.** Holiday, 1994.

Miller, Jay. **American Indian Festivals.** Children's Press, 1996.

Powell, Suzanne. **The Pueblos.** Franklin Watts, 1993.

Organizations and Online Sites

Anasazi Indian Village State Park
http://www.infowest.com/ anasazi/index.html

State park site that discusses the Anasazi civilization.

Early Man of Utah
http://www.surweb.org/ surweb/sandbox/teachers/ nmehs.htm

This site concentrates on the ancestors of modern tribes in the Southwest.

The Heard Museum: Native Cultures and Art
http://hanksville.phast. umass.edu/defs/ independent/Heard/

Museum site that exhibits American Indian Art in the Southwest.

Indian Pueblo Cultural Center
http://www.viva.com/nm/ PCCmirror/PCC.html#toc

This site provides links to the nineteen individual Pueblo groups.

Murals of the Indian Pueblo Cultural Center
http://hanksville.phast.umass. edu/defs/independent/ PCC/murals.html

A site of several colorful Pueblo murals.

Native American Navigator
http://www.ilt.columbia. edu/k12/naha/nanav.html

A general site with hundreds of links to topics on Native Americans.

Pueblo Cultural Center
2401 12th Street NW
Albuquerque, New Mexico 87192
Cultural center dedicated to the heritage of the Pueblos.

New Mexico's Cultural Treasures
http://www.nmculture.org/

A central index listing the museums, monuments, and natural wonders of New Mexico.

45

Important Words

ancestors people who came before

clan collection of families living together

irrigation ditch dug-out trench that allows water to reach crops

kachina special dancer who imitates the spirits

kiva underground chamber where special ceremonies take place

piki thin bread

potter person who works with clay to make pots or bowls

succotash mixture of beans and corn

turquoise blue-green stone prized by Zuni jewelers

Index

Meet the Author

Alice Flanagan thinks of the world as an open book filled with living stories. As an author, she thinks of herself as an observer—one who watches the stories as they unfold, then carefully writes them down.

Once a teacher, Ms. Flanagan taught Native American children in South Dakota and New Mexico. She feels blessed by the wonderful gifts they shared. Now, through her writing, she tries to pass these gifts on to others. In the True Book: Native Americans series, Ms. Flanagan is the author of the following titles. *The Eskimo, The Chippewa, The Navajo, The Nez Perce, The Pueblos, The Shawnee, The Sioux, The Tlingit, The Utes, The Wampanoags,* and *The Zunis.* Ms. Flanagan lives with her husband in Chicago, Illinois.

Photo Credits ©: Joe LeMonnier: 6; North Wind Picture Archives: 4, 18, 20, 26, 28, 29, 32; Reinhard Brucker: 1, 12, 13, 22 top, 35 right, 36 bottom, 39; Smithsonian Institution, National Anthropological Archives: 9; Stephen Trimble: cover, 2, 10,15, 22 bottom, 25, 31, 33, 35 left, 36 top, 40, 43 bottom inset, 43 top.